A Short Primer on How to Evaluate Health Promotion Programs

Michael P. O'Donnell, MBA, MPH, PhD

AMERICAN JOURNAL *of*

Health Promotion

This workbook is published by the American Journal of Health Promotion, P.O. Box 1254, Troy, Michigan 48099-1254. For additional information email contact@healthpromotionjournal. com.

CONTENTS

PURPOSE, SCOPE AND FORMAT

The purpose of this workbook is to provide a short guide on how to evaluate a workplace health promotion program. It addresses the value of program evaluation, types of evaluation, methodology to conduct outcomes evaluation, and strategies to conduct the evaluation. For a more detailed review of methods, readers are referred to the chapter titled Workplace Health Promotion Program Evaluation, in *Health Promotion in the Workplace*, 4th edition.[1]

IMPORTANCE OF EVALUATION

The primary purposes of program evaluation are to measure how well programs are being implemented and what results they are producing. If done in a timely fashion, this allows the program to be reshaped to better achieve objectives, and ultimately to ensure that scarce resources are being used in the most cost effective manner to achieve these objectives. Program evaluation efforts that are well designed can also make a contribution to the field's knowledge base by publishing information about how programs can be conducted to achieve the best outcomes and the magnitude of impact that can be expected.

TYPES OF EVALUATION

Structure, process, and outcome evaluation are the three basic types of evaluation. An important companion to outcome evaluation efforts is measuring the interrelationship of important variables within the program. Examples of these analyses are described later in the workbook.

Structure Evaluation

The purpose of structure evaluation, sometimes called formative evaluation, is to determine how well a program is structured to achieve program goals. Important questions include the following:

- Are goals articulated clearly?
- Are the appropriate programs being offered to achieve these goals?
- Are the appropriate staff in place to deliver these programs?
- Is an appropriate evaluation plan in place to measure outcomes?

The structure of a program is at least as important as the actual interventions in improving the health of employees or controlling medical costs. As such, structure evaluation should be conducted as a program is being launched and periodically, perhaps every two years.

The HERO Scorecard and the CDC Worksite Health ScoreCard are two tools developed to help employers conduct structural evaluations of programs and are available in the public domain. Brief descriptions of these scorecards are in the Appendix.

Process Evaluation

The purpose of process evaluation is to determine if the program is being implemented as planned. Important questions include the following:

- Have funds been allocated to support the program as planned?
- Have staff been hired and trained as planned?
- Is the program being offered to people according to schedule?
- Are programs being promoted as scheduled?
- Are health screenings measuring the intended health factors?
- Are skill building programs teaching the intended skills?
- Are facilities being constructed as planned?
- Are people signing up for and completing programs as planned?

Process evaluation should be conducted as a program is being implemented, and periodically, especially when program outcomes are not as good as expected.

Outcome Evaluation

The purpose of outcome evaluation is to determine the impact of a program. The most basic outcomes flow from process evaluation: levels of participation for the various program components and levels of satisfaction for major program elements.

The next level of outcome evaluation usually focuses on changes in health-related knowledge, behaviors and health conditions. Changes in knowledge might include better understanding of how to manage stress or prepare nutritious foods. Changes in behaviors might include increases in physical activity levels, improved eating habits, and quitting smoking. Changes in health conditions might include losing weight, reducing stress, controlling blood pressure, and reducing cholesterol.

The most advanced level of outcome evaluation might focus on changes in the organization's culture, reduction of medical costs, or enhancement of productivity.

Interrelationship of Variables

A close cousin to outcome evaluation is studying the interrelationship of important variables related to the program. These analyses might include measuring the relationship between modifiable health risks and medical costs, describing how health risks and medical costs change over time independent of a health promotion program and measuring how medical costs change as risks change. Examples of these types of analyses are described at the end of the workbook.

Qualitative versus Quantitative Evaluation

Quantitative evaluation focuses on numerical outcomes like the numbers of people quitting smoking, medical costs saved, etc. These are the "hard" statistics that many top managers and scientists need in order to have confidence that a program is working. Qualitative research focuses on subjective measures like testimonials, focus groups, and interviews with program participants; it provides a context that helps to explain why programs are working well or not. It provides the human perspective that helps to make the statistics relevant to real life. Stories from program participants about how they gained a new awareness about the importance of healthy lifestyle, shared new information with a family member, made progress in a behavior change, felt a new sense of energy, or made some other positive change can help other employees connect with a program and be more interested in participating. Testimonials that describe how a program impacted a person's life can be very powerful in securing long term support for a program. The testimonial in Exhibit 1 was sent in by an employee who joined a health promotion program managed by the author. It was gratifying to the program staff, increased their resolve to work in this field and reinforced the importance of the program among top management.

Exhibit 1: *Testimonial from program participant*

"I am sending you this note from the hospital. I was involved in a horrendous car crash. I will be in the hospital for a long time and will have months of therapy after I am discharged. But I am alive. When I joined your program, I decided to make one important change. I am not a health nut. I still smoke. I do not exercise very often and I eat more junk food than I should. The change I made was to buckle my seat belt every single time I got in a car. I am alive because of you. I thank you. My mother thanks you."

Triangulation involves a combination of qualitative and quantitative research, and is the ideal approach in any comprehensive program evaluation. Triangulation allows the statistics to come alive by showing the human perspective. For example, the quantitative analysis of a fitness program would show how many participants improved their cardiovascular capacity, strength and flexibility, and by how much. The qualitative analysis would help explain why people did or did not achieve positive outcomes. For example, to what extent did people respect the instructor, enjoy spending time with each other, have trouble fitting the program into their schedules, feel energized or exhausted by sessions, or sustain injuries?

Most of the comments on methodology in this workbook are relevant primarily to quantitative analysis for outcomes evaluation.

SETTING REALISTIC EXPECTATIONS

It is important to set realistic expectations for program outcomes, so top managers and employees are not disappointed by the outcomes that are achieved. For example, the most successful smoking cessation programs achieve a long term quit rate of about 35%, which probably sounds very low to a typical manager (See more details below). Without prior knowledge of likely quit rates, a manager might expect much higher quit rates and discontinue funding of a program achieving quit rates in this range. It is very difficult to make a simple statement about the level of outcomes that are realistic in terms of program participation or changes in knowledge, health behaviors, health conditions, or productivity enhancements, because the conditions are different in every organization. For example, some programs are well designed, well funded, and well implemented, while other programs are too superficial to expect any positive outcomes. Furthermore, very little research has been conducted to determine normal ranges for the many outcomes measured in a program. Most importantly, outcomes will primarily depend upon the quality of program provided, which is in turn dependent upon top management support, program budget, quality of marketing efforts, size and ability of program staff, and quality of individual programs offered. Best case scenarios have been developed in several areas. Some of these are discussed below.

Program Budgets

A benchmarking study conducted by the author in the late 1990's found that programs with the best health and financial outcomes had annual budgets that translate to $250–$350 per person in 2013 dollars and one full time staff person for every 2000 employees.[2]

HRA participation

Studies by Taitel and Seaverson found that participation in health risk assessment questionnaires are typically in the 20% range, but can reach 40% with strong management support and excellent marketing. If financial incentives of approximately $200 per person are implemented well, participation rates can reach 70%. When incentives are integrated into health plan premiums, participation rates have reached the 90% level.[3,4]

Tobacco Cessation Rates

A comprehensive review of 27 meta-analyses of thousands of tobacco cessation efforts has estimated the quit rates of a wide range of behavioral and medication therapy programs with surprising precision. It concluded that the optimal number of minutes of behavioral therapy is 300, the optimal number of therapy sessions is 8, the optimal mix of staff is a physician plus two other professionals, and the optimal intervention is a combination of a physician giving brief advice to quit and referring a patient into a program that includes behavior therapy plus the form of medication determined by a professional to be optimal for that patient. Under ideal conditions, success rates can approach 35%, compared to rates as low as 5% for people who try to quit on their own.[5]

Medical Care Cost and Absenteeism Reduction

A meta-analysis of well-designed studies on the financial impact of health promotion programs found an average savings in medical costs of $3.27 for every dollar invested and $2.73 of savings in reduced absenteeism.[6] These savings were achieved by some of the most well-designed programs and this level of savings should not be expected for the typical program. A systematic review of a broader range of studies on the impact of 47 workplace health promotion programs found that 46 programs saved money, 41 saved money in excess of their costs, with returns on investment ranging from -3.3 to 28.71.[7]

Other program outcomes

A systematic review of the literature by Soler et al found strong or sufficient evidence to conclude that well-designed comprehensive health promotion programs that include health screening plus feedback plus skill building are likely to produce improvements in tobacco use, dietary fat consumption, blood pressure, cholesterol, absence from work, seat belt use, heavy drinking, physical activity, health risk score, and medical utilization, but not for improved fitness, weight loss or improved fruit and vegetable consumption.[8] The level of improvement in each area from a population prevalence perspective is shown in Exhibit 2.

Exhibit 2: *Level of Evidence on the Effectiveness of Programs involving Health Assessment with Feedback Plus Skill Building by Program Focus*

<u>**Conclusion: Strong evidence of effectiveness**</u>

Tobacco use (30)	- 1.5 % population prevalence	
Dietary fat consumption (11)	- 5.4 % population prevalence	- 2.3 % consumption
Blood Pressure co ntrol (31)	- 4.5 % population prevalence	
Cholesterol management (36)	- 6.6 % population prevalence	- 4.8 mg/dl
Absence from work (10)		- 1.2 days/year less

<u>**Conclusion: Sufficient evidence of effectiveness**</u>

Seat belt use (10)   - 27.6 % population prevalence
Heavy drinking (9)   - 2.0 % population prevalence
Physical activity (18)   -15.3 % population prevalence
Health risk score (21)
Medical utilization (7)

<u>**Conclusion: Insufficient evidence of effectiveness**</u>

Fitness (9)	positive outcomes	small effect sizes, multiple measures
Body composition (27)		
- BMI (8)	-.5 BMI unit	consistent findings
- Weight (17)	-.56 pds	small effect size
- Fat (6)	-2.2 %	small effect size

<u>**Conclusion: Not effective**</u>

Fruit and vegetable consumption (8)   minimal changes observed

*Numbers of studies are shown in parentheses ( )

Source: Solar RE, Am Jour Prevent Med 38,2,2, 2010

METHODOLOGY FOR OUTCOMES EVALUATION

The quality of a study of program outcomes is determined by the structure of the study, validity and reliability of the measures, appropriateness of the sample, and appropriateness of the analysis of the data. Each of these concepts is described briefly below.

Study Structure

The structure, or design, of a study is the framework under which measurements of study outcomes are collected.

Posttest Only

The most common and least valuable structure is the **posttest only** design, in which a program is provided and then the measurement is collected. For example, a fitness program is offered, and then fitness levels are measured. This design is fine for measuring program satisfaction, or collecting testimonials, but not very useful for most outcomes because there is no baseline against which to measure changes.

Pretest/Posttest

The **pretest/posttest** design involves a measurement before and after the program is implemented. For example, participant's weight is measured before and after a weight control program. The two measurements make it possible to determine how much weight each person lost during the time of the program. This study design is of limited value because it does not measure enough to determine if the change in weight was caused by the program, or by other influences in the people's lives. For example, the weight loss may have been caused by the opening of a fitness center at work, or more healthy food served in the cafeteria at work. The pretest/post test study design is acceptable for measuring health outcomes from individual health behavior change program offerings (like quit smoking, stress management, weight control, etc.) after the optimal approach has been established through rigorous research and when a program is implemented following the same protocols. The posttest only and pretest/posttest structures are considered *non-experimental designs*.

Pretest/Posttest Structure with a Comparison Group

A **pretest/posttest structure with a comparison group** structure involves measuring change for the group of people who participate in the program and those who do not. This structure is called a *quasi-experimental design*. For example, in a quit smoking course, smoking rates would be measured for a group of people who participated in a program and a similar group of smokers who chose not to participate in the program. The weakness of this design is that it does not account for differences in age, gender, ethnicity, motivation or other factors between the groups. For example, the people who joined the quit smoking program were motivated to join the program. It is possible that motivation was enough to stimulate quitting. Maybe the motivated people would have quit without the program. The bias introduced by levels of motivation can be reduced by measuring levels of motivational readiness to change, perhaps in health risk assessment questionnaires completed by participants and non-participants and included as control factors in the analysis. The most practical approach to controlling for these factors is to measure age, gender, ethnicity, readiness to change, and other factors that may influence success in changing a behavior, and then use statistical methods to control for differences in these factors between the treatment and comparison groups. The more sophisticated approach to control for these factors is called propensity score matching, in which a comparison group is assembled from all the non-participants by identifying non-participants who match participants in all of the important characteristics. This is possible only when the number of participants is very large and data on the important characteristics are collected automatically, independent of the health promotion program. For example, it is not unusual for an employer to have information on age, gender, job type, other demographic information, and medical claims for many employees. The employer may also have information on health risks, and readiness to change for employees who have completed a health risk questionnaire or health screening.

Experimental Design

The quasi-experimental study design provides the minimal level of rigor necessary to provide any confidence in findings related to the impact of programs on medical cost. To better overcome the potential selection biases not controlled for in the *quasi-experimental design*, an **experimental design** can be developed in which people are randomly assigned to the treatment and no treatment (or control) conditions. For example, smokers who want to quit are randomly assigned to participate in a quit smoking program or to a wait list for a future quit smoking program. The difference in quit rates between the two groups shows the effect of the program. If smokers quit on their own, without the program, it shows that motivation was enough to get them to quit. If they quit only when they join the program, it shows that the program was necessary for them to quit. Note: when the group not receiving treatment is selected through random assignment, it is called a "control" group. If assignment is not random, it is a "comparison" group.

Solomon Four Group

One of the limitations of the experimental design, the *pretest/posttest with random assignment* is that measuring the behavior might motivate a person to change. This might occur after someone goes through a health screening and discovers an unknown health condition. A more elaborate study design, called the **Solomon Four Group**, controls for the possible impact of measurement by randomly assigning people to four different groups. The first group is measured, participates in a program, and is then measured again. The second group is measured at the same time intervals but does not participate in the program. The third group is measured at the first measurement point, but not the second, and the fourth group is measured at the second measurement point, but not the first. This study design might be used on drug studies, but has probably never been used in a health promotion program and is described here only to show the extent to which study designs can be refined to improve rigor.

Time Series or Longitudinal Analysis

Another way to control for motivation and other factors is the **time series** or **longitudinal analysis**, in which multiple measures are taken before and after a program is offered. This allows a pattern to be established in the absence of a program. This is especially important for medical costs, which tend to increase for people as they age, and as level of risk fluctuates in the absence of a program. The time series approach can be used in a non-experimental design if there is no comparison group, in a quasi-experimental design if there is a comparison group that is not randomly assigned, or an experimental group if there is a randomly assigned control group. The most rigorous study design that is feasible in a workplace setting is probably a quasi-experimental time series analysis in which three years of medical cost data is collected before the program is implemented and changes in values for program participants are compared to non-participants who have been matched to participants by propensity scoring. It may be possible to conduct a randomized controlled time series analysis with propensity score matching to test the impact of a program, but this crosses the line between program evaluation to research, and the cost of the research might exceed the cost of the program. People who advocate randomized controlled trials as the gold standard for evaluating the financial impact of workplace health promotion programs do not have an advanced level of understanding of workplace health promotion, research methodology, and more importantly, do not understand the purpose of program evaluation or why employers evaluate their programs. Of the 47 studies on the financial impact of workplace health promotion programs that have been published in peer reviewed scientific journals, 9 are randomized controlled trials, 21 are quasi-experimental designs, 10 are non-experimental designs, and 7 are models built on reported associations.[7]

The study designs described above are illustrated graphically in Exhibit 3.

Measures

In most program evaluation efforts, it is not feasible to have a direct measure of the actual knowledge, behavior, or health outcome being targeted. For example, if the program goal is to improve the eating habits of employees, the ideal measurement of eating habits would be to monitor all the food an employee consumes for an extended period of time. This, of course, is not practical. The alternative is to ask employees to fill out a questionnaire describing the foods they eat. Similarly, if the goal were to reduce stress, the ideal would be to somehow peer into a person's mind, sense the level of stresses they are exposed to and observe how they handle stressful situations for an extended period of time. This also is not practical. A practical alternative is to ask employees to fill out a questionnaire describing their exposures and reactions to stress, and symptoms of not being able to handle stress.

The alternative measure, such as a questionnaire, is useful only to the extent that it is valid and reliable. Validity is the extent to which the measurement does indeed measure what it is intended to measure. Reliability is the consistency of those measures in repeated measurements. **Validity** is determined by comparing the alternative measurement against a "gold standard." For example, the gold standard for determining the amount of fat on a person's body (i.e. body fat percentage) is hydrostatic weighing. In hydrostatic weighing, a person blows all of the air out of their lungs, and is submersed under water. The amount of water they displace and their weight is measured. These values are entered into formulas to determine body fat. The formulas were developed based on dissections of human corpses. Hydrostatic weighing is not unusual with elite athletes, but is not practical for most people, especially in workplace health promotion programs. As such, alternative measures have been developed, including measuring the thickness of fat at various spots on the body, electrical impedance, the bod pod and others. These estimates of body fat

Exhibit 3: *Evaluation Structure or Design*

NON-EXPERIMENTAL DESIGNS

- One Group Posttest Only

$$X \qquad O_2$$

- One Group, Before and After (Pretest-Posttest Only)

$$O_1 \qquad X \qquad O_2$$

QUASI-EXPERIMENTAL DESIGNS

- Pretest and Posttest with Comparison

$$O_1 \qquad X \qquad O_2$$

$$O_1 \qquad\qquad O_2$$

EXPERIMENTAL DESIGNS

- True Experimental

$$O_1 \qquad X \qquad O_2$$
[R] _____
$$O_1 \qquad\qquad O_2$$

- Solomon Four Group

$$O_1 \qquad X \qquad O_2$$
_____
$$O_1 \qquad\qquad O_2$$
[R] _____
$$O_1$$
_____
$$O_2$$

LONGITUDINAL OR TIME SERIES ANALYSIS DESIGNS

- Single Longitudinal or Time Series

$$O_1 \quad O_2 \quad O_3 \quad O_4 \quad X \quad O_5 \quad O_6 \quad O_7 \quad O_8$$

- Multiple Time Series

$$O_1 \quad O_2 \quad O_3 \quad O_4 \quad X_1 \quad O_5 \quad X_2 \quad O_6 \quad X_3 \quad O_7 \quad O_8$$

Key:

$O_1, O_2, \ldots$ = Observations or recording of behaviors, test scores or other phenomenon

X = Health Promotion Intervention

------- = Lack of random assignment to treatment and control conditions

[R] _____ = Random assignment of subjects to treatment and control conditions

percentage are compared against those of the hydrostatic weighing for the same people to determine their validity. Similarly, the *reliability* of a measurement tool is determined by repeating these measurements on the same person several times and comparing the results. A very reliable measure gets the same results each time. There are several types of validity and reliability,[9] but they are not reviewed here because of space limitations.

The simplest way to ensure that a measure is a valid and reliable measure is to use standardized measures that have already been tested for validity and reliability. Thousands of questionnaires have been developed to measure almost every psychological and physical construct imaginable. Some of these are in the public domain and are free to all users. Others are proprietary and must be purchased.

One of the most common measurement tools for an individuals' health in workplace health promotion programs is the health risk assessment or HRA. HRAs typically consist of 40–80 questions on a wide range of health habits, biometric measures, medical conditions, and health interests. Most of them have algorithms that help the individual user understand the impact of current health habits on future health, and provide suggestions on how to improve health. Aggregate reports provided to management combine the data from all the individual respondents to illustrate trends and highlight insights. The best HRAs are validated against mortality[10] and medical costs.[11,12] For example, tests of the HRA of the Health Management Research Center at the University of Michigan have shown that the difference between the chronological age and the risk age are associated with the 20 year death rates of men and women (exhibit 4), the components that make up the wellness score (health risks, mortality risks and use of preventive services) have comparable associations for age groups ranging from under 44 to over 75, (exhibit 5), that these have similar associations with medical costs (exhibit 6), and the wellness score is correlated with medical costs (exhibit 7).

Exhibit 4: *Validity Of The Health Risk Appraisal To Predict 20 Year Chances Of Dying (1959–1979) In The Tecumseh Community Health Study*

Actual Age Minus Risk Age	20 Year Death Rates (Percent)	
	Males	Females
+2 to +5	0.0	3.0
−1 to+1	2.8	2.8
−5 to −2	9.8	8.9
−0 to −6	29.0	15.5
< −10	36.2	30.5
Total	19.3	8.9
From Foxman and Edington, Am. J. Pub. Health 77:971–974, 1987		

M | HEALTH MANAGEMENT RESEARCH CENTER
UNIVERSITY OF MICHIGAN

Exhibit 5: *Contribution of Component Scores to Total Wellness Scores by Wellness Levels and Age*

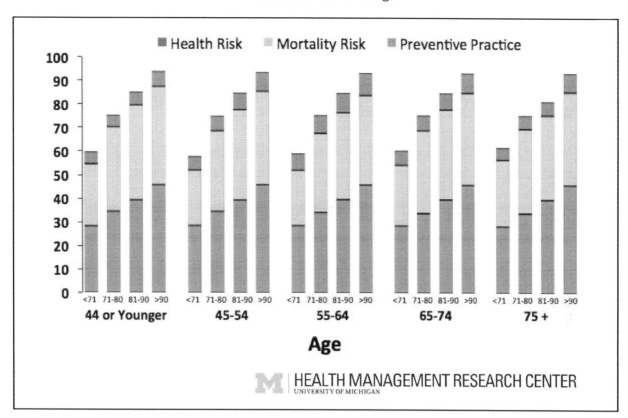

Exhibit 6: *Contribution of Component Scores to Total Medical Care Costs by Wellness Levels and Age*

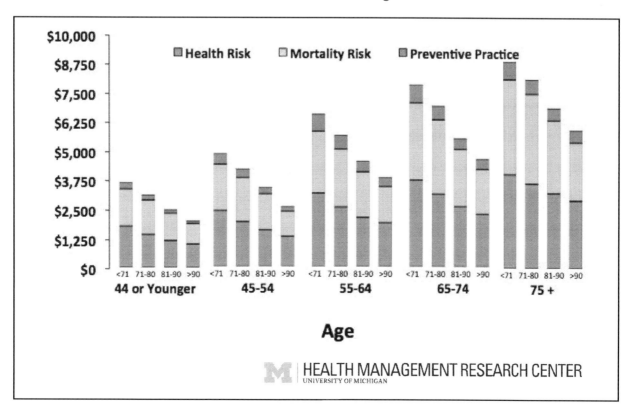

Exhibit 7: *Relationship Between Annual Medical and Pharmacy Costs and HRA Wellness Score*

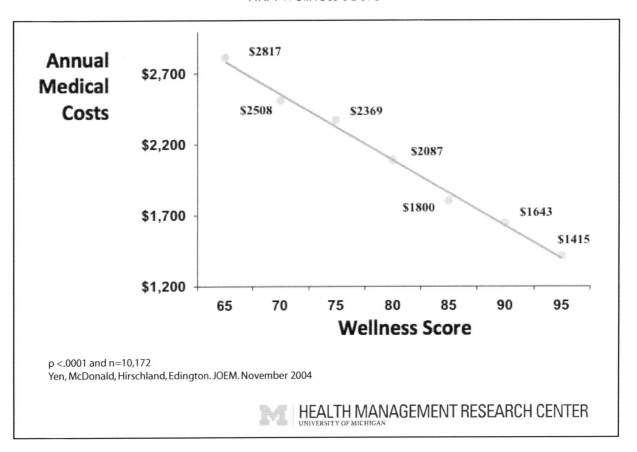

p <.0001 and n=10,172
Yen, McDonald, Hirschland, Edington. JOEM. November 2004

M | HEALTH MANAGEMENT RESEARCH CENTER
UNIVERSITY OF MICHIGAN

Another common measure of physical health is a health screening that measures blood pressure, height and weight, cholesterol, glucose or hemoglobin A_1c, and sometimes triglycerides. These tests can be performed easily at a low cost and are important predictors of heart disease and diabetes. Values from health screenings can be entered into HRAs by the individuals, or through a data load directly into the electronic record of the HRA.

Study Sample

It is not possible to collect data for an evaluation from 100% of the target population in most worksite health promotion programs. In some cases, funds might not be available to provide health screenings for all employees. In most cases, some employees may choose not to participate in a health screening or complete and submit an HRA. When fewer than 100% of eligible employees participate, it may or may not be possible to generalize the findings from those who participate to the full population. Two factors are important: representativeness and sample size.

A sample is **representative** of, or similar to, the full population if it is similar to the full population in ways that influence whatever is being measured. For example, blood pressure is often influenced by gender, weight, nutrition, physical activity, emotional stress, presence of another medical condition and family history. Smoking status is often influenced by age, education, ethnicity, and country of residence. It is often not possible to know the values of all these factors for people who do not complete the health screening or the HRA, so analysts typically try to compare values that are easier to collect, including age, gender, education, and location of residence. If the sample and the full population are very different from each other, it is not prudent to generalize findings from the sample to the full population. It may be possible to adjust findings of the sample to account for differences with the full population, but this is effective only to the extent that known differences influence the variables of interest.

One way to ensure that the sample is similar to the full population is to intentionally select the sample through a random selection process, and then compare the sample with the full population on the known characteristics.

If the sample is sufficiently similar to the full population, either because of random selection, or similarity of the known traits, the **size** of the sample must be considered before findings are generalized to the full population. The formula for determining sample size necessary for any population size is shown in Exhibit 8. For a study population of only 100 people, a sample size of 79 is needed. However, for a population of 1000, only 278 are needed, and for a population of 10,000, only 370 are needed, if the sample is representative of the full population.

Exhibit 8: *Sample size formula*

$$n = (z^2 \, PQ) \div (e^2 + z^2 \, PQ \div N)$$

n = sample size

z = standard normal deviate corresponding to the acceptable Type I or false positive error, a situation in which the analysis shows a difference between two groups when such a difference really does not exist. .05 is a normally accepted value, in which case z = 1.96.

P = the portion of the population who have the trait being studied, for example the portion who smoke cigarettes.

Q = the portion of the population who do not have the trait being studied, for example the portion who do not smoke cigarettes.

e = confidence interval; ± 5% is often an acceptable confidence error

N = the size of the full population

Analysis

Most employers prepare descriptive statistics to report the prevalence of the health risks they track. They analyze this data to detect trends over time, especially improvements in their areas of priority. One of the common challenges in analysis is matching the statistics to the distribution of data. For example, most medical cost utilization data is not normally distributed. Typically, most people have very low costs, and a small number of people have high costs. When data is not normally distributed, parametric statistics, the most common statistical analyses, including means, Students t test, and ANOVA cannot be used. These data need to be transformed before comparable analysis can be conducted, or non-parametric statistics must be used. A complete description of the types of statistical analysis conducted is beyond the scope of this short workbook.

TYPICAL EVALUATION STRATEGIES

No Evaluation Efforts

The vast majority of employers who sponsor health promotion programs, especially small employers, do not conduct formal structure, process or outcome evaluations of their programs. They rely on the informal feedback of employees who participate in their programs. Given the low cost of a health promotion program, even when it is comprehensive, this approach may be tempting for programs that do not need to justify costs to top management, especially for programs that do not have clearly articulated goals. Indeed, most businesses do not conduct formal evaluations for expenditures of similar or larger magnitude. For example, a comprehensive health promotion program costs about $250–$350 per employee per year, about the same cost as interior decorating, or landscaping; businesses rarely evaluate expenditures for interior decorating or landscaping in any formal manner. Similarly, most employers spend more maintaining their equipment than they do on their health promotion program, and they rarely conduct a formal evaluation on those expenditures. As such, most employers conclude they do not need to conduct a formal evaluation of their wellness program. This approach is very short sighted because it results in little or no documentation of the program, no way to determine if the program is having any effect or if resources are being used in a cost effective way.

Compare Health Risk Assessment (HRA) Over Time

The most common strategy among employers who do conduct a formal evaluation of their health promotion program is to rely on the aggregate reports generated from HRAs, and monitor changes over time. The best HRAs provide a detailed breakdown of risk levels for different parts of the organization, quantify changes over time, and use proprietary algorithms to link changes in risks with changes in medical costs. This type of aggregate analysis is normally provided at little or no additional cost beyond the base cost of the HRA. This type of analysis is valuable only to the extent that a large portion of the employees complete the HRA on an annual basis. The accuracy of the connection between changes in risks and changes in medical costs is limited by the extent to which these relationships for the employer track with those of the HRA provider, and the validity of the HRA. Employers typically supplement the HRA analysis with testimonials and tracking participation. If the HRA is the primary tool used to measure the financial impact of the program, it is critical that the HRA be validated against medical costs.

In-depth, longitudinal analysis

Several hundred large employers have decided to conduct in-depth, longitudinal analyses of their health promotion programs. The typical approach is to collect individual-level data on demographics and health risks from HRAs and health screenings, participation in health promotion programs, medical, pharmacy, disability, productivity, and other costs, and send the data to an independent third party expert for storage and analysis. The third party expert protects the privacy of the data, retains the data over a period of years, and uses advanced statistical methods to provide aggregate level analysis and reporting back to the employer. This approach makes sense for large employers who place a high priority on discovering the most effective health promotion strategies and focusing their resources on efforts that are the most cost effective in improving health, reducing medical costs and enhancing productivity. Another advantage of this approach is that it protects the privacy of the individual employee. The employer never sees individual-level data, only an aggregate-level summary and trends. Different types of analyses are conducted at different stages of evolution of the program. Exhibit 9 shows the types of analyses that might be conducted at each stage.

Exhibits 10, and 11 illustrate analyses that can be performed after health risk data are collected but before programs are offered. Exhibit 10 shows that health care costs increase as age increases and also as numbers of health risks increase, to the extent that a person 35–44 with high risks (5 or more) has greater costs than a person 65–74 with low risks (0–2). Similarly, exhibit 11 shows that employees with 3–4 and 5 or more health risks have medical costs $1261 and $3321 higher than those with 0–2 risks.

Exhibit 9: *Types of Evaluation Efforts at Different Stages of Program Maturity*

Pre-implementation
- Medical cost trends
- Natural transitions in medical costs categories
- Excess medical costs linked to health risks
- Factors associated with medical costs

Early Implementation
- Health risks associated with short term disability incidence
- Participation rate by location
- Self reported health conditions associated with on-the-job work loss
- Prevalence and distribution of employee health risks
- Prevalence and distribution of employee health risks: Top 3 prioritized risks
- Early impact of program on OSHA incidence rates
- Early impact of program on weight
- Changes in the natural flow of medical costs

Intermediate Implementation
- Early indications of program impact on risk status
- Early indications of program impact on medical costs
- Early indications of program impact on illness absenteeism

Mature Program
- Return on investment (ROI)
- Award applications
- Custom studies

Exhibit 10: *Medical Costs Associated with Age and Number of Risks*

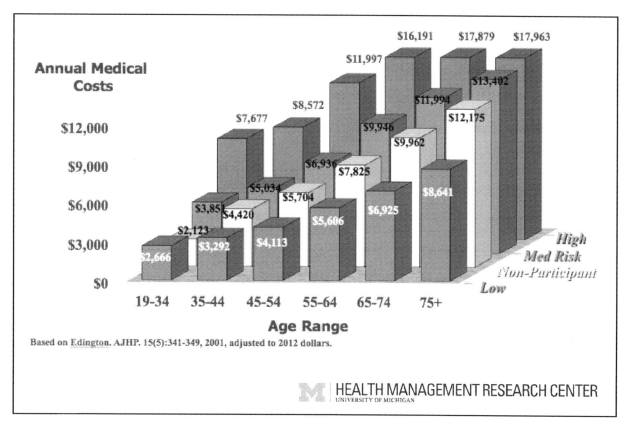

Based on Edington. AJHP. 15(5):341-349, 2001, adjusted to 2012 dollars.

HEALTH MANAGEMENT RESEARCH CENTER
UNIVERSITY OF MICHIGAN

Exhibit 11: *Excess Medical Costs Associated with Excess Risks*

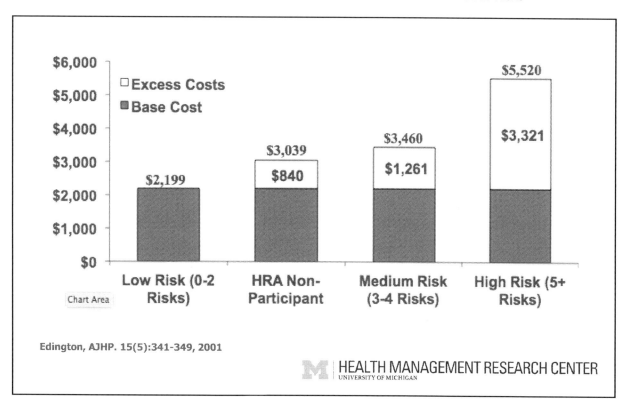

Edington, AJHP. 15(5):341-349, 2001

HEALTH MANAGEMENT RESEARCH CENTER
UNIVERSITY OF MICHIGAN

Exhibits 12 and 13 illustrate analyses than can be performed several years after the program is in place. Exhibit 12 shows that costs decrease as numbers of risks decrease, and costs increase by a greater amount as risks increase. Exhibit 13 shows that costs for those who make health improvements increase slightly over time, but increase substantially for those who do not make improvements.

Finally, Exhibit 14 shows the financial return on investment (ROI) achieved by an organization over a series of years.

These types of analyses might cost $50,000 for a single analysis, and several hundred thousand dollars for a comprehensive analysis for a large employer.

Exhibit 12: *Change in Medical Costs Associated with Number of Changes in Risks*

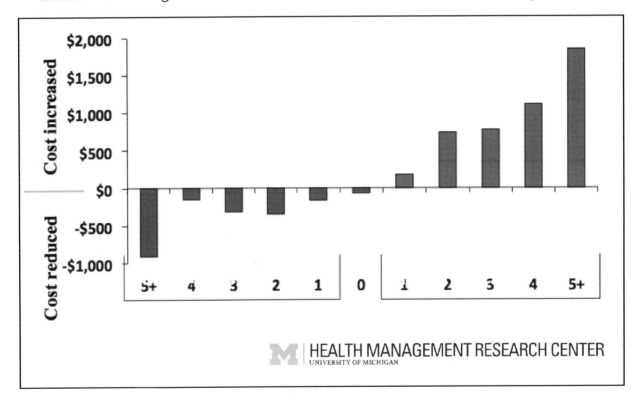

Exhibit 13: *Changes in medical costs among employees who improved or did not improve*

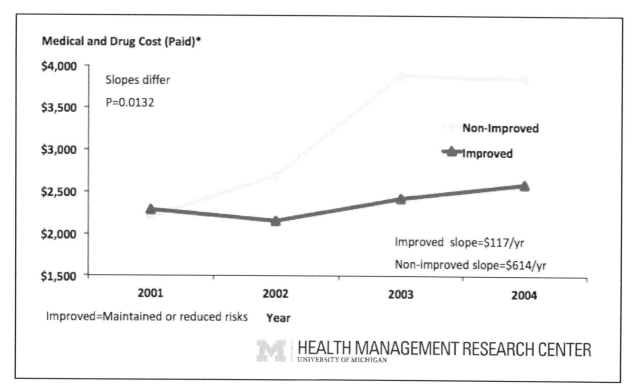

Exhibit 14: *Return on Investment in multiple years*

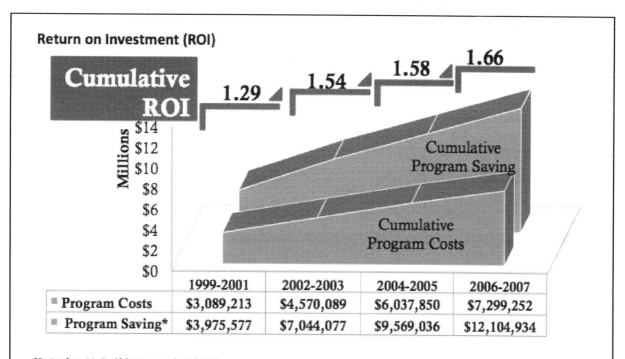

	1999-2001	2002-2003	2004-2005	2006-2007
Program Costs	$3,089,213	$4,570,089	$6,037,850	$7,299,252
Program Saving*	$3,975,577	$7,044,077	$9,569,036	$12,104,934

*Saving from Medical/pharmacy and productivity

Source: Yen L, Schultz AB, Schaefer C, Bloomberg S, Edington DW. Long-term return on investment of an employee health enhancement program at a Midwest utility company from 1999 to 2007. *International Journal of Workplace Health Management.* 2010; 3(2): 79-96

References

1   Goetzel RZ, Health Promotion in the Workplace Program Evaluation. In O'Donnell, MP (Ed), *Health Promotion in the Workplace, 4th edition. 2015. Troy, MI: American Journal of Health Promotion.*

2   O'Donnell M, Bishop C, Kaplan K. Benchmarking best practices in workplace health promotion. *Art of Health Promotion.* March/April 1997;1:1.

3   Taitel MS, Haufle V, Heck D, Loeppke R, Fetterolf D. Incentives and other factors associated with employee participation in health risk assessments. *J Occup Environ Med.* 2008;50(8):863–72.

4   Seaverson EL, Grossmeier J, Miller TM, Anderson DR. The role of incentive design, incentive value, communications strategy, and worksite culture on health risk assessment participation. *Am J Health Promot.* 2009; 23(5):343–52.

5   Fiore MC, Jaen CR, Baker TB, et al. Treating Tobacco Use and Dependence: 2008 Update. Clinical Practice Guideline. Rockville, MD: U.S. Department of Health and Human Services. Public Health Service. May 2008.

6   Baicker KM, Cutler D, Song Z. Workplace wellness programs can generate savings. *Health Affairs.* 2010;29:304–311.

7   Baxter S, Sanderson K, Venn AJ, Blizzard CL, Palmer AJ. The Relationship Between Return on Investment and Quality of Study Methodology in Workplace Health Promotion Programs, Am J Health Promot, 2014;28(6): 347–363.

8   Soler RE, Leeks KD, Razi S, et al. A systematic review of selected interventions for worksite health promotion: The assessment of health risks with feedback. *Am J Prev Med.* 2010;38(2S):S237–S262.

9   Carmines EG, Zeller RA. Reliability and Validity Assessment, Beverly Hills, CA: Sage; 1997

10 Foxman , Edington DW. The accuracy of health risk appraisal in predicting mortality. Am. J. Pub. Health. 1987; 77:971–974.

11 Yen L, McDonald T, Hirschland D, Edington DW. Association between wellness score from a health risk appraisal and prospective medical claims costs. J Occup Environ Med. 2003;45(10):1049–57.

12 Yen, LT Edington DW, Witting P. Associations between health risk appraisal scores and employee medical claims costs in a manufacturing company. Am J Health Promot. 1991;6(1), 46–54.

13   HERO Best Practice Scorecard in Collaboration with Mercer. Available at: http://www.the-hero.org/scorecard_folder/scorecard.htm. Accessed September 18, 2013.

14   Centers for Disease Control and Prevention. *The CDC Worksite Health ScoreCard: An Assessment Tool for Employers to Prevent Heart Disease, Stroke, and Related Health Conditions.* Atlanta: U.S. Department of Health and Human Services; 2012. Available at: http://www.cdc.gov/dhdsp/pubs/worksite_scorecard.htm. Accessed September 18, 2013.

Appendix

I. HERO SCORECARD

The HERO Best Practice Scorecard © was developed as a tool to help employers improve the quality of their health promotion programs by documenting program components, primarily from a management perspective. The Scorecard can be used as an inventory to catalogue a program's components, an indicator of success in implementing program components and as a comparative benchmarking tool to compare a program with peer employers. HERO has published several reports summarizing findings drawn from the database of responses.

In version 4.0, the core questionnaire has 64 questions organized into six major sections: 1) strategic planning (7 questions), 2) organization and cultural support (8 questions), 3) programs (14 questions), 4) program integration (6 questions), 5) participation strategies (21 questions), and measurement and evaluation (8 questions). It also has optional sections on program costs, outcomes, outcome measures, and financial impact.

Users complete the Scorecard online. A report is sent to the user showing the score for their organization and average scores for all other organizations.

The Scorecard was developed through a collaborative process involving several dozen leading authorities in health promotion who volunteered their time and expertise to HERO (Health Enhancement Research Organization), and Mercer who provided expertise in health promotion and technical support to produce the tools.

The Scorecard and a follow-up report with scores for the individual user organization and average aggregate scores for all other organization users are provided at no charge to all users. More detailed reports with aggregated responses for each question, breakdowns of scores by industry, geographic region, and employer size can be purchased.

More details can be found at HERO Scorecard website:[13] http://www.the-hero.org/scorecard_folder/scorecard.htm.

II. THE CDC WORKSITE HEALTH SCORECARD: AN ASSESSMENT TOOL FOR EMPLOYERS TO PREVENT HEART DISEASE, STROKE, & RELATED HEALTH CONDITIONS

The CDC Worksite Health ScoreCard[14] was developed to help employers determine if they have implemented evidence based interventions and strategies. It focuses primarily on the components of individual program interventions but includes a short section on organization level design.

The questionnaire contains 100 questions that assess the extent to which evidence-based strategies have been used in programs. The strategies include counseling services, environmental supports, policies, health plan benefits, and other worksite programs shown to be effective in preventing heart disease, stroke, and related health conditions. The 100 questions are organized into 12 major sections: organizational supports (18 questions). tobacco control (10 questions), nutrition (13 questions), physical activity (9 questions), weight management (5 questions), stress management (6 questions), depression (7 questions), high blood pressure (7 questions), high cholesterol (6 questions), diabetes (6 questions), signs and symptoms of heart attack and stroke (4 questions) and emergency response to heart attack and stroke (9 questions). Users tally their own scores manually and there is no mechanism to contribute scores to a central database.

All of the items in the questionnaire are tied to strategies that have been documented in the scientific literature to be effective. From a scoring perspective, the relative value of each item is weighted to reflect both the magnitude of impact of the approach and the quality of published evidence supporting its impact. References to the scientific literature are provided for each topic area. The questionnaire was field tested with a sample of 93 very small, small, medium, and large worksites for validity and reliability, and feasibility of adopting the strategies highlighted in the tool.

The Appendix includes an example of the strategies, processes, communications and evaluation elements that might be in a plan to achieve several specific health goals. It also includes sample program budgets, and blank templates that can be used to prepare plans and budgets.

The CDC Scorecard was developed by a team of professionals at CDC and Emory University. It was released in September of 2012. More information can be found at The Worksite Health Scorecard website: http://www.cdc.gov/dhdsp/pubs/worksite_scorecard.htm

Made in the USA
San Bernardino, CA
27 November 2017